[UNDERSTANDING GRAMMAR]

VERBS *and* ADVERBS

ANN RIGGS

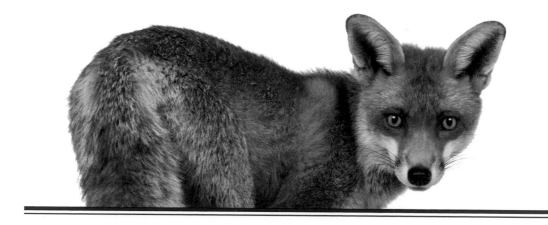

CREATIVE ● EDUCATION

Published by Creative Education
P.O. Box 227, Mankato, Minnesota 56002
Creative Education is an imprint of The Creative Company
www.thecreativecompany.us

Design and production by Liddy Walseth
Art direction by Rita Marshall
Printed by Corporate Graphics in the United States of America

Photographs by Corbis (Bettmann, Christie's Images, Trolley Dodger, Jason Horowitz,
Photo Collection Alexander Alland, Sr.), Mick Ellison, Getty Images (Michael Blann,
Dave King, Life On White, Sharon Montrose, Steve Morenos/Newspix, Hitoshi Nishimura,
Christoph Rosenberger, Joel Sartore, Gail Shumway, Kim Taylor, Judy Unger,
Freudenthal Verhagen, Maarten Wouters), iStockphoto (Arlindo71, Jill Battaglia,
Emmanuel Hidalgo, Eric Isselée, Leontura, Arpad Nagy-Bagoly, Jon Patton, Edyta Pawlowska,
Victor Zastol Skiy)
Illustration on page 5 © Etienne Delessert

Library of Congress Cataloging-in-Publication Data
Riggs, Ann.
Verbs and adverbs / by Ann Riggs.
p. cm. — (Understanding grammar)
Includes bibliographical references and index.
Summary: An examination of the rules behind English grammar, focusing on the components
known as verbs and adverbs, which name and describe the action or state of being
necessary to compose sentences.
ISBN 978-1-60818-096-7
1. English language—Verb. 2. English language—Adverb. 3. English language—Grammar. I. Title.
II. Series.

PE1271.R54 2010
428.2—dc22   2010028303

CPSIA: 110310PO1386

First Edition
2 4 6 8 9 7 5 3 1

TABLE of CONTENTS

4

INTRODUCTION

CHAPTERS

6

The Verb Is the Word

14

Crossing over or Not

22

Strategies for Irregular Verbs

30

Characteristic Qualities

36

Modifying Action and More

BUILD YOUR OWN SENTENCE ACTIVITIES

12

Seeing Clearly, Saying Correctly

20

Be Objective about This

28

All by Myself

34

Writing Is Tense!

44

What's in the Daily News?

46

GLOSSARY

47

SELECTED BIBLIOGRAPHY

48

INDEX

Music swells. Siblings squabble. Owls hoot. I am. Grammar is.

And just like that, two words can become a SENTENCE. The information in a short sentence can be expanded by adding more words that give vivid descriptions or specific reactions. Where should those words be placed? How does a writer know what PUNCTUATION to use? What does all of that mean, anyway? Words fall into place more easily when one has an understanding of grammar, a system of rules that gives writers the foundation for producing acceptable, formal expression. It is that acceptable form, that appropriate grammar, which helps readers comprehend what has been written.

We are indebted to the Romans, who conquered most of Europe from 75 B.C. through the first century A.D., for spreading the term *verbum* along with the rest of their Latin vocabulary. *Verbum* is the source of our word "verb," and it means "word." Truly, without a verb, every sentence is doomed. All sentences have a subject and a verb. The verb is the main element of the predicate, the part of the sentence that tells something about the subject. We define the verb, this hub of a sentence, as a word or group of words that expresses the action or indicates the state of being of the sentence's subject. That suggests that the verb is either *doing* some-

[4]

thing (acting), or it is *existing* (that it just *is*). Even when the subject of a sentence may be understood (not written in the sentence), a verb is mandatory, as in the one-word sentence "Think!"

Our word "adverb" connects the Latin PREFIX *ad-*, meaning "to" (expressing an addition to), with *verbum*. From that association we get the PART OF SPEECH that describes or modifies verbs, ADJECTIVES, or other adverbs. Adverbs add character to the words they describe by restricting or intensifying their meaning, as in the words *gently, yesterday, there,* and *ultimately*. What else makes adverbs important in our sentences? Degrees of comparison that give writers ways to expand their descriptions from *quieter* to *loudest* and from *more nervous* to *most entertaining*—these are adverbs, too. When writers accurately use verbs and the words that describe them, readers have no trouble following along.

THE VERB IS ~ THE WORD

Verbs have basic PRINCIPAL PARTS that produce all their forms. The four principal parts are present, present participle, past, and past participle. These parts tell the TENSE of the verb. Present tense happens today, and the present participle shows something is happening right now. Although the past form happened yesterday, the past participle with an AUXILIARY indicates what happened at a previous time in the past or will happen in the future. Most verbs are regular, meaning that they form their present participles with the suffix (or ending) -*ing* and their past participles with the suffix -*ed* plus an auxiliary verb. When an auxiliary verb is used with a main verb, it is called a helping verb. Spelling of the main verb may necessarily change when adding -*ing*. See Table 1 for

examples of auxiliary verbs used with main verbs and Table 2 for specific changes in regular verb forms.

Even though most verbs are regular, the culprits that don't follow the rules, the irregular verbs, are another story. Verbs that are irregular do not take the usual form and have these considerations: 1) They may not change at all from present to past and past participle. 2) They may change for only the past and past participle. 3) They may use a different word entirely for present, past, and past participle. The best way to keep irregular verb forms straight is to memorize them. Dictionaries list them with each verb's definition. Some examples are shown in Table 3 on page 8.

The verbs in Tables 2 and 3 have this in common: the present and past forms—whether

AUXILIARY/ HELPING VERBS

am	is	are	was	were	be	being	been
has	have	had	do	does	did	can	could
shall	should	will	would	may	might	must	ought

TABLE 1

REGULAR VERBS

PRESENT MAIN VERB FORM	PRESENT PARTICIPLE AUXILIARY + MAIN + ING	PAST MAIN + ED	PAST PARTICIPLE AUXILIARY + MAIN + ED
laugh	am/is/are laughing	laughed	has/have/had laughed
learn	am/is/are learning	learned	has/have/had learned
pretend	am/is/are pretending	pretended	has/have/had pretended
sneak	am/is/are sneaking	sneaked	has/have/had sneaked
suppose	am/is/are supposing	supposed	has/have/had supposed

TABLE 2

regular or irregular—never need a helping verb; they can stand alone. See? *Saw* needs no help(er). The tables also show the main verbs plus their helping verbs in the present and past participial forms. Under certain circumstances, though, auxiliaries may be the only verbs present in the sentence, instead of functioning as helpers. In his story "All Gold Canyon" (1905), American author Jack London (1876–1916) recounts a confrontation between a prospector, or a miner looking for gold, and a claim jumper who tries to steal the prospector's claim. How many times does London use the verb *was* in the following excerpt? Can you identify when it is the only verb and when it is the auxiliary used with present and past participles?

IRREGULAR VERBS

PRESENT MAIN VERB FORM	PRESENT PARTICIPLE AUXILIARY + MAIN + ING	PAST	PAST PARTICIPLE AUXILIARY + PAST FORM
am/be	is/are being	was/were	has/have/had been
lay (to put or place)	is/are laying	laid	has/have/had laid
lie (to recline)	is/are lying	lay	has/have/had lain
lie (to make a false statement)	is/are lying	lied	has/have/had lied
raise	is/are raising	raised	has/have/had raised
rise	is/are rising	rose	has/have/had risen
see	is/are seeing	saw	has/have/had seen
set	is/are setting	set	has/have/had set
sit	is/are sitting	sat	has/have/had sat
take	is/are taking	took	has/have/had taken

TABLE 3

" The next instant the stranger felt the miner's hand grip his wrist. The struggle was now for the revolver. Each man strove

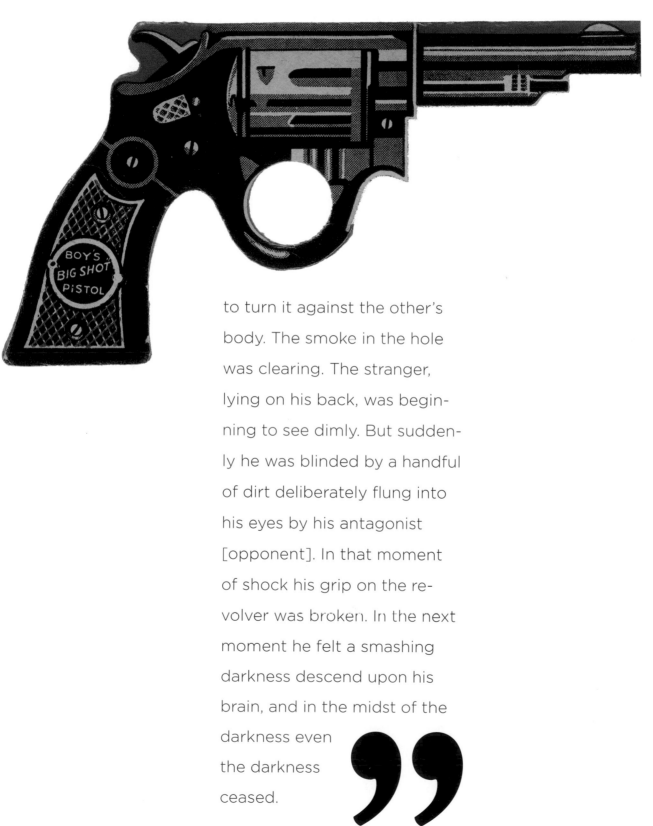

to turn it against the other's body. The smoke in the hole was clearing. The stranger, lying on his back, was beginning to see dimly. But suddenly he was blinded by a handful of dirt deliberately flung into his eyes by his antagonist [opponent]. In that moment of shock his grip on the revolver was broken. In the next moment he felt a smashing darkness descend upon his brain, and in the midst of the darkness even the darkness ceased. "

The past tense word *was* in sentence two is the only verb: **The struggle *was* now for the revolver.** But in four other sentences it is used as an auxiliary: ***was* clearing, *was* beginning, *was* blinded**, and ***was* broken.** Notice how the use of the present participles (*clearing, beginning*) and the past participles (*blinded, broken*) changes the focus of the action from present to past tense, even with the same past tense helping verb. The actions of the smoke that ***was* clearing** and of the stranger who ***was* beginning to see** are shown a noun complement that renames the subject or a word called an adjective complement that describes it. Because these complementary words occur in the predicate, they are also known as predicate nouns (or predicate nominatives) and predicate adjectives. Compare the following two sentences: **Today is Wednesday. Atlas is strong!** In the first sentence, the subject, "today," is linked to the predicate noun, "Wednesday." In the second sentence, "Atlas" is described by a predicate adjective, "strong." Both sentences use the

ATLAS IS STRONG!

as having begun sometime in the past but continuing into the present, while the instances in which the helper and past participles are used (***was* blinded** and ***was* broken**) make it plain that the action is over.

A linking verb links—or joins—the subject of the sentence to its complement, a word or phrase in the predicate part of the sentence that further identifies or explains it, completing the sense of the subject. That means that the linking verb is followed by either a word called same linking verb, *is*. Linking verbs just exist; they have no action, but they bridge the gap between subjects and their complements. Table 4 shows words often used as linking verbs.

LINKING VERBS

am	is	are	was	were	be	being	been
feel	look	smell	sound	taste	appear	become	fall
get	grow	prove	remain	run	seem	stay	turn

TABLE 4

Helping verbs (Table 1) are used with action verbs, as in this sentence: **I *am* pretending,** when the action verb, "pretending," needs the helper, *am*. Did you notice some of the same words in both Tables 1 and 4? At times they're used as linking verbs with subject complements, as shown in this sentence: **I *am* ecstatic!** The predicate adjective, "ecstatic," describes "I," the subject, and the verb, *am*, serves as the link. Many times, helping verbs are also used with linking verbs, such as **It *does seem* possible.**

Seeing Clearly, Saying Correctly

Sometimes verb errors are hard to correct because they're hard to find, but mistakes below have been placed in italics. Use a dictionary to find the four principal parts of each present tense form and write them down on your paper. (You'll find *was* listed with *am* in Table 3 on page 8.) Rewrite the paragraph, correcting the grammar as you check the sentences for subject-verb agreement.

We had a good time at the beach last weekend. After we had *ate* our sandwiches and had drunk our sodas, we played baseball. We were too near the water, though, and after the ball had been *threw* in several times, we *growed* tired of it all and dived in ourselves. The wind *blowed* steadily, and the water was very cold; so even before we had *swam* 10 minutes, we had to come out. I *run* a race along the beach with Bill, who was almost *froze*. You should have *saw* us when we got home, though—we *was* covered with sand!

ANSWER KEY

CROSSING OVER OR NOT

Verbs in sentences with a subject, an action verb, and a DIRECT OBJECT are known as transitive verbs. The action transfers—or goes across the verb—from the subject to the direct object. Deciding whether a sentence has a direct object is easy. After locating the action verb—being certain the verb shows action, such as "drive," "melt," or "take," and is not a state of being verb, as with "is," "was," and "were"—ask yourself *whom* or *what*. If a noun or PRONOUN object completes the thought, the verb is transitive, as in this sentence: **The trucker drives his rig 2,000 miles (3,219 km) each week.** Drives what? A rig. Why is knowing about the transitive verb important? The direct object that receives the action of the verb acts as an object complement, as it completes the thought that the subject and verb begin. Writers want to finish what they start; direct objects of transitive action verbs do just that. Let's consider a literary example involving two main characters in American writer Henry Sydnor Harrison's 1911 short story, "Miss Hinch." One character is a clergyman, and the other is described as "her" or "the woman."

 The clergyman's eyes followed her candidly, and watched her sink down, presently, into a seat on his own side of the [subway] car. A young couple sat between them now; he could no longer see the woman, beyond occasional glimpses of her black knees and her faded bonnet, fastened on with a long steel hatpin.

HE

Reducing the sentences to their basic parts gives us subjects, action verbs, and direct objects. In sentence one, the subject is *eyes*, the action verbs are *followed* and *watched*, and the direct object is *her*. To check to see if we identified the direct object correctly, we can ask, "The eyes followed whom or what?" The answer is "her." In the second sentence, look at the second part after the punctuation mark called a semicolon (;): subject (*he*), action verb (*could see*), direct object (*woman*). Again, we can check the direct object by asking, "He could see whom or what?" He could see the "woman." The direct objects help the reader focus on the woman being watched.

Intransitive verbs do not have a direct object, so a sentence with an intransitive verb may or may not have action. The sentence may be complete in itself or have additional words to explain what action—if any—happened, but no noun or pronoun object receives or is affected by the action. However, that doesn't diminish the impact of the verb—or of the sentence. Let's return to "Miss Hinch" and look at a section of the story that preceded our first excerpt.

HER

"An express was just thundering in, which the clergyman, handicapped as he was by his clubfoot and stout cane, was barely in time to catch. He entered the same car with the woman and chanced to take a seat directly across from her. It must have been then after twelve o'clock, and the wildness of the weather was discouraging to travel. The car was almost deserted. Even in this underground retreat the bitter breath of the night blew and bit, and the old woman shivered under her shawl. At last, her teeth chattering, she got up in an apologetic sort of way, and moved toward the better protected rear of the car, feeling the empty seats as she went, plainly in search of hot pipes."

Analysis of the corresponding subjects and verbs contained in that excerpt shows more evidence of intransitive verbs than transitive ones. How can we tell? We'll look for the direct objects—or the lack of them. See Table 5 for a breakdown of each.

TRANSITIVE OR INTRANSITIVE

SENTENCE	SUBJECT	VERB	WHOM/WHAT?	DIRECT OBJECT?	TRANSITIVE/ INTRANSITIVE
1	express	was thundering	(nothing)	no	Intransitive
2	he	entered	car	yes	Transitive
		chanced	(nothing)	no	Intransitive
3	It	must have been	(nothing)	no	Intransitive
	wildness	was discouraging	(nothing)	no	Intransitive
4	car	was	(nothing)	no	Intransitive
5	breath	blew	(nothing)	no	Intransitive
		bit	(nothing)	no	Intransitive
	woman	shivered	(nothing)	no	Intransitive
6	she	got	(nothing)	no	Intransitive
		moved	(nothing)	no	Intransitive

TABLE 5

Precise intransitive action verbs—such as *was thundering, chanced, blew, bit, shivered,* and *moved*—hold the reader's interest by keeping the focus on sentence subjects.

Be Objective about This

Imagine that you have been selected to choose one thing representing your country to send to an international exhibition, or fair. Using complete sentences, write specific reasons to explain your choice of object. Be sure that some of your verbs are transitive active, since your item is a direct object. Perhaps you'll choose one of these: a significant governmental document, a piece of music by your favorite composer, an artistic creation in sculpture or of classic literature, a rare plant, or animal. Or will you, unique individual that you are, go yourself?

STRATEGIES FOR IRREGULAR VERBS

An understanding of a transitive verb and its direct object versus an intransitive verb that doesn't have one can help in distinguishing between troublesome verb pairs. Three irregular verb pairs that are often misused are *sit/set*, *lie/lay*, and *rise/raise*. Their separate principal parts, included in Table 3, show the correct forms. However, the misinterpretation goes beyond knowing what word needs to be used with an auxiliary verb. Inaccuracies in writing also occur because of questions about transitive and intransitive use. One of each pair (*set*, *lay*, and *raise*) has to have a direct object following it because it is a transitive verb. A look back at Table 3 on page 8 shows the forms of *set*: "set, setting, set, set." In the sentence **Francie is *setting* the table,** the verb is transitive because if you ask, "Francie is setting whom or what?" the answer is the direct object, "table." Whenever you want to express an action of putting or placing an object, use *set*. In contrast, refer to Table 3 for the present, present participle, past, and past participle forms of the intransitive verb *sit*. Now consider the following sentences:

Present: I *sit* on the bus on my way to school.

Present Participle: Mark *is sitting* in his assigned seat.

Past: Yesterday I *sat* on the bus.

Past Participle: I *have sat* in the same bus seat each day all year.

Asking yourself, "sit, sat, or have sat whom or what?" doesn't make sense in these cases. There are no direct objects, only action. When you want to express an action that does not have a direct object, use a form of *sit* instead of *set*. Is this sentence correct? **I *set* on the bus for two hours.** No, it isn't. You *sat* there.

Similarly, confusion exists in the choice of *lie* or *lay*. When you want to convey the meaning of "reclining," as when a nurse instructs someone to **lie on the examination**

table, the patient acts all by himself. Lie what? There is no plausible answer; the patient just lies down. Therefore, the verb is intransitive. This can also be shown in the past tense using the following sentence: **Last night Ryan *lay* on his bed for an hour before falling asleep.** Ryan reclined on his bed all by himself. True enough, *bed* is an object, but in this sentence it serves as the object of the preposition *on* in the PREPOSITIONAL PHRASE *on his bed*. Our asking, "Ryan reclined what?" doesn't give a direct object answer, since he didn't recline anything other than himself, so the verb is again proven to be intransitive. Telling someone ***Lay* down over there** will always be wrong because the present tense verb *lay* means "to put or place" and needs a direct object. Instead, say ***Lie* down over there.** For the sentences **Please *lay* (put) the packages on the counter** and **Juan is *laying* the packages on the counter,** asking, "lay what?" and "is laying what?" returns the answer "packages," the direct object, both times.

Now for the third pair of problematic irregular verbs: how to tell the difference between the intransitive *rise* and transitive *raise*. First, recall the forms of *rise*: "rise, rising, rose, risen." In the present tense, an instruction such as **Please *rise* when your name is called** is correct because the subject (understood to be you) can *rise* all by himself. Similarly, in an illustration of the present

TENSIONS ROSE

participle, **Be sure the bread dough *is* not *rising* too fast,** the dough is just *rising* by itself; no one is *raising* it. For the past tense, it might be said, **When the players tied the score of the basketball game, tensions *rose*.** That's it. Tensions *rose*. We can confuse ourselves a bit and ask, "What rose?" The answer: tensions. But that's not the correct question form to use when trying to find a direct object; it only confirms that the action happened. Our question is always verb first, then *what,* as in, "Rose what?" Nothing fits. This proves there was no object of the action, only a subject, *tensions*.

Continuing our discussion of the past participle, a sentence such as **The temperature *has risen* above 90 °F (32 °C) since noon** shows that the temperature *has risen* all by itself. We can try to ask, "Has risen what?" But this doesn't make any sense, because it doesn't help us find an *object* of the action—which the sentence doesn't have. When speaking of the verb *raise,* we're concerned with *raise* in the sense of "lifting or being lifted" that has a direct object to receive its action. Note how, for the following examples in each tense, the question "Raise what?" will have an answer, meaning that the verb is transitive.

Present: The teacher told the students, "Please *raise* your hand if you have a

question." Raise what? Hand.

Present Participle: The soldiers *are raising* the flag. Raising what? Flag.

Past: Rex *raised* so many tomatoes in his garden that he began giving them away to anyone who would take them. Raised what? Tomatoes.

Past Participle: The enthusiastic students *have raised* all the money necessary for their trip to New York City. Have raised what? Money.

To summarize the difference between transitive and intransitive, imagine that during an English class verb study, a teacher writes on the chalkboard: I sit. I lie. I rise. One of the students surprises herself when she catches the

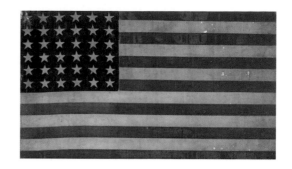

similarities *and* the significance, exclaiming, "*I* get it! If the verb has an *i* in it, *I* do it myself!" That is precisely the point for those particular intransitive verbs. A sentence using an intransitive verb has no direct object to receive its action. It may be complete in itself or have additional words to explain what happened, but, unlike a transitive verb, no object receives it; it does it by itself.

I GET IT!

BUILD YOUR OWN SENTENCE
All by Myself

Troublesome irregular verbs need to be separated by their principal parts and by their use (or lack of use) with direct objects. Look at page 8 for the forms of *rise* and *raise*, and write them on a sheet of paper. After that, add two items to the following lists of things that can rise all by themselves and two more that can be raised by something else. Write

a complete *rise/raise* sentence about each of the 10 items. Remember, in intransitive *rise* sentences, your choices will be subjects, but since *raise* is transitive, the items you choose will be direct objects. Might some items be on both lists?

THINGS THAT RISE:
GASOLINE PRICES
HELIUM BALLOONS
THE SUN

THINGS THAT ARE RAISED:
PETS
VEGETABLES
TEST SCORES

CHARACTERISTIC QUALITIES

Now that we can tell the difference between regular and irregular, auxiliary and linking, and transitive and intransitive, we can assess the five properties of all verbs: VOICE, tense, NUMBER, PERSON, and MOOD. Knowing the voice of a verb (active or passive) helps a writer choose the most effective verb form. In sentences with active voice verbs, the subject does the acting, as in this sentence: **Rod *slammed* on the brakes when he *saw* the deer directly in front of him.** Good writers typically consider active voice more forceful than passive voice, because it keeps sentences from becoming too complicated and focuses on who is performing the action. Passive voice always includes a form of the verb *to be* (am, is, are, was, were, be, being, been), and something else acts upon the subject, as in this sentence: **The brakes *were slammed* on by Rod when the deer *was seen* directly in front of him.** Did you notice that active voice is not only more direct, but it is also less wordy? Whether you choose active or passive, be sure to make the voice the same for all verbs in a sentence, and use the voice that is best suited to making the subject clearly understood.

Sometimes the passive voice is preferable when a writer wants to highlight the importance of a subject. In the active voice, the following sentence places the emphasis on the actor, the scientist: **The scientist *will present* data to confirm his hypothesis.** However, if it's the *data* that is crucial, not the presenter, the passive form would be more appropriate: **Data *will be presented* to confirm the scientist's hypothesis.** Another good reason for passive voice is demonstrated by the example above. What if you have no clue who is going to make the presentation? Using passive voice, the fact that data is going to be presented

TO

can still be confirmed. Passive voice can also lend a more objective tone to such documents as lab reports, as in the finding that states, **Population density *is* positively *correlated* with incidence of disease.** However, for the most part, when you want to be as clear as possible and use fewer words, active voice is the more efficient choice.

Though they may differ in how they form their past participles, both *action* and *being* verbs use tense to delineate when things occur. All verbs have three SIMPLE TENSES: present (happening right now), past (already happened), and future (to happen in a time yet to come). Future tense verbs require an auxiliary verb, such as *will* or *shall*: **Clarice**

will buy **a digital camera next week.**

Things get a bit stickier with what grammarians call the PERFECT TENSES. Each simple tense is also associated with one of the perfect tenses. These time frames come before or after another action and require the use of the main verb's past participle plus an auxiliary verb. (See Tables 2 and 3 for examples showing this formation.) For instance, present perfect tense explains action that began in the past and continues—either directly or in effect—into the present: **Suzie *has e-mailed* me every day for two years.** What began two years ago is still going on. We might compare that with simple present tense and say, **Suzie *e-mails* me every day.** But consider that sentence

BE

plus the additional information of how long the e-mailing has been going on: **Suzie *e-mails* me every day for two years.** Saying it that way not only doesn't make sense, it is also grammatically incorrect.

Let's take a look at another perfect tense. **Vince *had written* his book report, but he *forgot* to take it to school.** The sentence has two parts, each with its own subject and verb. This time the past tense helping verb *had*, combined with the past participle *written*, defines the verb tense in the first half of the sentence as past perfect. Along with the past form *forgot* in the second half, we have two actions that have been completed in the past. We don't have any problem figuring out which action happened first, though: 1) Vince wrote his report. 2) He forgot to take it with him. But using the past perfect tense makes the actions' timing more distinct by placing them in relation to each other.

The sixth basic tense is future perfect and refers to an action that *will have been* completed at some time in the future. It uses the auxiliaries *will* or *shall* and *have* with the past participle, as in the following example: **The winner of the contest *will have eaten* the most pies by the time the bell rings.** Neither the eating nor the ringing has yet occurred; however, we can be certain that both will at some point.

The third property of verbs is number. The verb must always agree in number (singular or plural) with its noun or pronoun subject, such as in the previous sentence, **The third *property* of verbs *is* number.** The subject, *property*, is singular and requires the singular verb *is*. Present and past participles and their helping verbs must agree in number as well as in the fourth property, person. Person refers to the speaker (first person—*I/we*), the person spoken to (second person—*you/you*), or the person spoken about (third person—*he/she/*

it/they). The singular forms *I, he, she,* and *it* need singular verbs, while plural forms *we* and *they* need plural verbs. Second person (*you*) always uses a plural verb, whether one or more than one person is spoken to. See Table 6 for a further breakdown of how person and number affect the choice of a singular or plural verb.

The fifth and final property of verb use is mood, which itself can be broken into three categories: indicative (expressing a fact or question), imperative (giving a command), and subjunctive (relating a condition or a wish). Good writers achieve variety of expression by manipulating the mood of their verbs. Look for the different moods in the following sentences:

Indicative: The bank closed before three o'clock on Tuesday.
Imperative: (the subject is understood to be "you") Deposit your check at the bank.
Subjunctive: If the bank were open, I would deposit my check.

When the mood is subjunctive and the verb is an auxiliary of *to be*, the form called for is *were*, not *was*. That's why this is correct: **If I *were* feeling better, I'd go to the mall.** However, when a statement *might* be true but isn't a certainty, use the indicative rather than the subjunctive form, as in the following: **If the cigarette lighter *was* the arsonist's, the fire marshall might have a solid case against him.**

PERSON AND NUMBER OF THE VERB

	SINGULAR	PLURAL
first person present tense	I am	we are
second person present tense	you are	you are
third person present tense	he/she/it is	they are
noun with present tense verb	parakeet whistles	parakeets whistle
first person present participle	I am being	we are being
second person present participle	you are being	you are being
third person present participle	he/she/it is being	they are being
noun with present participle	mallard is swimming	mallards are swimming
first person past tense	I was	we were
second person past tense	you were	you were
third person past tense	he/she/it was	they were
noun with past tense verb	swallow migrated	swallows migrated
first person past participle	I have/had been	we have/had been
second person past participle	you have/had been	you have/had been
third person past participle	he/she/it/ has/had been	they have/had been
noun with past participle	duck has/had been seen	ducks have/had been seen

TABLE 6

BUILD YOUR OWN SENTENCE
Writing Is Tense!

Some people like to do only what they already do well. Other people try new things and take risks. Which do you prefer? Write complete sentences to explain your viewpoint in three paragraphs, taking care to give specific reasons and examples. Use past tense to tell about an experience you once had. Then explain how that event affects your present life. Because the past and present may help you reach a goal, also tell about your future, using future tense for what you hope will occur. Be sure to keep the verb tense consistent with your meaning. Table 6 may give you some help with the tenses.

MODIFYING ACTION AND MORE

An adverb can modify a verb, an adjective, or another adverb by showing the relation of manner (how), time (when), place (where), degree (how much or to what extent), and reason (why) of the words being described. Many adverbs end in *-ly*; however, appearances can be deceiving. We must not assume that all words ending in *-ly* are adverbs. Some are verbs, such as **Rally the troops!** Others are adjectives, as in **He's in an *ugly* mood.** Generally, adverbs do not follow the linking verb forms of *be*, *seem*, *smell*, *appear*, *feel*, *become*, *taste*, *hear*, and *look*. In such cases, the modifier is linked to the subject rather than to the verb. For instance, **Roger *felt* fine when he woke up.** *Fine* describes Roger, not *felt*, and adverbs cannot modify nouns. Do we care? We must care if we want to write well. Linking verbs are tricky. When talking about someone's health, referring to how ill the person appears or feels, use the adverb *well*: **I don't think Sally looks *well*.** When talking about a person—modifying a noun or pronoun—use the adjective *good*: **He looks *good*!** Adjectives, not adverbs, modify nouns and pronouns.

Sir Arthur Conan Doyle (1859–1930) wrote a mystery story featuring his famous detective, Sherlock Holmes, called "The Adventure of the Speckled Band" in 1892. In the following short conversation between Sherlock Holmes and his distraught client, Miss Helen Stoner, five adverbs describing two of the most common relationships (manner and degree) can be identified: *very*, *absolutely*, *most*, *certainly*, and *too*.

"It is very essential, Miss Stoner," said he, "that you should absolutely follow my advice in every respect."

"I shall most certainly do so," she replied.

"The matter is too serious for any hesitation. Your life may depend upon your compliance."

A close examination of these adverbs illustrates their variety:

Very modifies the adjective *essential* and answers the question of degree, or how much. *Absolutely* modifies the verb *should follow* and answers the question of degree. *Certainly* modifies the verb *shall do* and answers the question of manner, or how. *Most* modifies the adverb *certainly* and answers the question of degree. *Too* modifies the adjective *serious* and answers the question of degree.

If Miss Stoner had merely said, "I shall do so," her reply would not have been nearly as effective. With each adverb, the seriousness of the situation grows. Yet even her addition of *most certainly* isn't enough to convince Sherlock Holmes that she fully understands the gravity of her situation.

To express quality, quantity, or manner, adverbs have three degrees, or levels: the positive, the comparative, and the superlative. Positive adverbs express one quality without reference to any other thing, as in **The baby's mother sang *softly*.** The comparative differentiates between the action or condition of two things, and there are two ways of forming this degree. Most one-syllable adverbs that do not end in *-ly*, as well as the adverb *early*,

form the comparative degree with *-er*: **The coach knew he could count on Zach to finish *earlier* than Jon; Zach runs *faster*.** Adverbs of more than one syllable usually form the comparative with the aid of *more* or *less*: **Carol studied *more thoroughly* than Rhonda, and her hard work paid off.** Even some tongue-twisters can be used adverbially to differentiate between two materials: **Lesser leather never weathered wetter weather better.** Superlative adverbs make a comparison among at least three things and are formed with the suffix *-est* or the words *most* or *least*, as shown in the following examples: **The *fastest* of the 10 relay teams will qualify for the state meet** and **Of the six presenters, Daphne argued her case *most effectively*.**

In spite of our best efforts to pigeonhole comparative and superlative degrees with *-er/more* and *-est/most*, some adverbs don't follow those clear-cut rules; their degrees are irregular. A few common irregulars in the positive degree are *well, badly, little* and *much*. See Table 7 for their comparative and superlative forms.

The words are completely different! What's more, there are other adverbs that don't have degrees at all; they cannot be compared. As such, these adverbs are known as absolute—complete in themselves. We cannot use *-er/-est* or *more/most* with these words: *always, eternally, now, essentially,* and *uniquely.*

IRREGULAR ADVERBS

POSITIVE DEGREE	COMPARATIVE DEGREE	SUPERLATIVE DEGREE
well	better	best
badly	worse	worst
little	less	least
much	more	most

TABLE 7

WELL BADLY LITTLE MUCH

"Miss Barry was a rather selfish old lady, if the truth must be told, and had never cared much for anybody but herself. She valued people only as they were of service to her or amused her. Anne had amused her, and consequently stood high in the old lady's good graces…. "If I'd [Miss Barry] a child like Anne in the house all the time I'd be a better and happier woman."

Anne and Diana found the drive home as pleasant as the drive in—pleasanter, indeed, since there was the delightful consciousness of home waiting at the end of it…. When she crossed the log bridge over the brook the kitchen light of Green Gables winked her a friendly welcome back…. Anne ran blithely up the hill and into the kitchen, where a hot supper was waiting on the table…. "Marilla, a broiled chicken! You don't mean to say you cooked that for me!"

"Yes, I did," said Marilla…. "I'm glad you've got back, I must say. It's been fearful lonesome here without you, and I never put in four longer days."

After supper Anne sat before the fire between Matthew and Marilla, and gave them a full account of her visit.

"I've had a splendid time," she concluded happily, "and I feel that it marks an epoch [a time of notable events] in my life. But the best of it all was the coming home."

Canadian author Lucy Maud Montgomery (1874–1942) wrote *Anne of Green Gables* in 1908. The story follows the journey of a precocious 11-year-old orphan, Anne Shirley, and her life with unmarried middle-aged siblings Matthew and Marilla Cuthbert. In the excerpt at left, Anne and her best friend Diana are leaving the home of Diana's great-aunt. The lonely Miss Barry evaluates her life, and Anne realizes where she belongs. Look for the adverb descriptors explaining how, when, where, and how much and for the adverbs (irregular and regular) that express degree.

In the first sentence, *rather* qualifies the adjective "selfish" in a comparative way, indicating Miss Barry is not as selfish as some other people. And the verb "had cared" has two adverb modifiers, *never* and *much*. All words that negate a verb, such as *not, never, no*, and the CONTRACTION for "not," *n't*, describe a verb. Although they are in the predicate, they are not verbs—they're adverbs. In sentence two, *only* modifies the verb, "valued," answering the adverb question, *How much?* In the third sentence, *consequently* begins a part of the sentence that cannot stand alone, while *high* answers the question *Where?* about the verb "stood." Miss Barry uses two *-er* comparative degree adverbs, *better* (irregular for "good") and *happier* (regular for "happy"), in the fourth sentence as she reflects on her otherwise lonely, unhappy existence.

Next, the adverb connecting words, *indeed*

RATHER NEVER MUCH NOT NO CONSEQUENTLY HIGH BETTER ALWAYS NOW

and *since* act as transitions between the two parts of the fifth sentence. How did Anne run up the hill in sentence seven? *Blithely*. In sentence nine, the *n't* in "don't" changes "do" to "do not," just as an adverb modifier does in a verb.

In sentence 12, Marilla's conversational expression, "*fearful* lonesome," is a way of comparing being lonesome and being really, really lonesome. That's how much she has missed Anne. Where has it been lonesome? *Here*. Other adverbs, *never* and *longer*, add degrees of comparison; *never* is the opposite of always; *longer* is comparing the length of Anne's being gone to how the time passes when she is home. In the next-to-last sentence, the *-ly* adverb *happily* shows how Anne concludes her account of the visit. While recounting the enjoyable time she had, Anne's delight in returning to her family is superlative: more than good or better; it is the *best* and is a fitting end.

No matter how many degrees, properties, or principal parts are involved, developing a better grasp of verbs and adverbs is worth your time. Choosing the exact vocabulary to transfer your thoughts to your readers' minds is a valuable investment, since how well you use verbs determines how well you write. Why keep trying to understand how action, state of being, and modifiers work together in sentences to create correct expression? The ready answer is so that others will recognize your writing as both grammatically acceptable and interesting, not as embarrassingly incorrect. For instance, if you say that the reader "should have *saw*" the connection you made about auxiliary and main verbs, your word choice may just ruin an otherwise good impression of your writing; it's something you should have *seen* coming. Keep studying verbs and the words that describe them, and above all, keep writing!

KEEP WRITING!

BUILD YOUR OWN SENTENCE
What's in the Daily News?

Newspaper headlines use subjects and verbs, even though they are not complete sentences. In trying to be brief, headline writers' efforts are sometimes unintentionally humorous, as in these examples:

"Squad Helps Dog Bite Victim"
"Red Tape Holds Up New Bridge"
"Man Struck by Lightning Faces
    Battery Charges"
"Kids Make Nutritious Snacks"

Imagine you're the reporter who has been assigned to write the story, taking any approach you choose, humorous or straightforward. Pick one of those headlines, and make up a story. In your first paragraph, answer the questions that subjects, verbs, and adverbs cover in all news items: Who? What?

When? Where? Why? Wrap up your story by answering the question, "What's next?" Use action verbs and active voice, and grab the reader's attention by using an opening question or an unexpected quote!

GLOSSARY

adjectives: words or groups of words that describe or modify nouns

auxiliary: a verb that provides additional help; sometimes also known as a helping verb

contraction: a shortened form of a word or group of words, with the missing letters usually marked by an apostrophe

direct object: the person or thing that receives the action of a transitive verb

mood: the property of a verb that expresses a statement or a question (indicative mood), a request or a command (imperative mood), or a condition or a wish (subjunctive mood)

number: the property of verbs, nouns, and pronouns identifying them as one item (singular) or more than one item (plural)

part of speech: the class or category into which a word may be grouped according to its form changes and its grammatical function; in English, the main parts of speech are verbs, nouns, pronouns, adjectives, adverbs, prepositions, conjunctions, and interjections

perfect tenses: the verb forms that represent time using a form of *have* in complex time relationships: present perfect (*has/have* found), past perfect (*had* found), and future perfect (*shall/will have* found)

person: the property of a verb (or noun or pronoun) that relates to the speaker (first person—*I/we*), the person spoken to (second person—*you/you*), or the person spoken about (third person—*he/she/it/they*)

prefix: an element at the beginning of a word that qualifies or changes the root word's meaning

prepositional phrase: a group of words consisting of a preposition (*at, by, of, to,* etc.), its object, and any modifiers

principal parts: the verb forms that indicate various tenses: present, past, and past participle (which is used with a helping verb)

pronoun: a word that substitutes for a noun

punctuation: marks used to provide meaning and separate elements within sentences, such as periods, commas, question marks, exclamation points, semicolons, colons, hyphens, and parentheses

sentence: a unit of expression that contains a subject and a verb and expresses a complete, independent thought

simple tenses: the verb forms that represent present, past, and future time

tense: the property of the verb that designates time as present, past, future, or perfect using single-word verbs and auxiliaries

voice: the property of the verb that shows that the form is either active (the subject is doing the action; the verb is transitive, leading to a direct object) or passive (the subject is the receiver of the action; the verb has no direct object and is intransitive)

SELECTED BIBLIOGRAPHY

The Chicago Manual of Style. 15th ed. Chicago: The University of Chicago Press, 2003.

Darling, Charles. "Guide to Grammar." Capital Community College Foundation. http://grammar.ccc.commnet.edu/grammar/.

Hodges, John C., Winifred B. Horner, Suzanne S. Webb, and Robert K. Miller. *Harbrace College Handbook*. 13th ed. Fort Worth, Tex.: Harcourt Brace College Publishers, 1998.

Hunter, Estelle B., ed. *The New Self-Teaching Course in Practical English and Effective Speech*. Chicago: The Better-Speech Institute of America, 1935.

Lederer, Richard, and Richard Dowis. *Sleeping Dogs Don't Lay: Practical Advice for the Grammatically Challenged*. New York: St. Martin's Press, 1999.

O'Conner, Patricia T. *Woe Is I Jr.: The Younger Grammarphobe's Guide to Better English*. New York: G. P. Putnam's Sons, 2007.

Strunk, William, and E. B. White. *The Elements of Style*. 4th ed. New York: Longman Publishers, 2000.

Warriner, John E., Joseph Mersand, and Francis Griffith. *English Grammar and Composition*. New York: Harcourt, Brace & World, Inc, 1963.

INDEX

action verbs 4, 11, 14, 16, 19, 31, 43, 44

adjectives 5, 36, 38, 41

    as distinguished from adverbs 36

adverbs 5, 36, 38, 39, 40, 41, 43, 44

    absolute 38, 40

    degrees of comparison 5, 38, 39, 40, 41, 43

        comparative 38, 39, 41, 43

        irregular 38, 39, 40, 41

        positive 38, 39

        superlative 38, 39, 43

    describing relationships 36, 38, 40, 43, 44

    fine vs. *well* 36

    -ly pitfalls 36

auxiliary verbs 6, 7, 8, 10, 11, 22, 30, 31, 32, 43

    use with main verbs 6, 7, 8, 10, 11, 31, 32, 43

contractions 41, 43

direct objects 14, 16, 19, 20, 22, 24, 25, 27, 28

    and complements 14, 16

Doyle, Sir Arthur Conan 36, 37, 38

    "The Adventure of the Speckled Band" 36, 37, 38

Harrison, Henry Sydnor 14, 15, 16, 17

    "Miss Hinch" 14, 15, 16, 17

helping verbs *see* auxiliary verbs

intransitive verbs 14, 16, 19, 22, 24, 25, 27, 29, 30

irregular verbs 6, 8, 22, 24, 25, 27, 28–29, 30

    common pairs of 22, 24, 25, 27, 28–29

linking verbs 10, 11, 30, 36

    and complements 10, 11

London, Jack 8, 9, 10

    "All Gold Canyon" 8, 9, 10

Montgomery, Lucy Maud 40, 41, 43

    Anne of Green Gables 40, 41, 43

mood 30, 32

    imperative 32

    indicative 32

    subjunctive 32

number 30, 32, 33

    and subject-verb agreement 32

person 30, 32, 33

    and choice of singular or plural verbs 32, 33

predicate adjectives 10, 11

predicate nominatives 10

predicates 4, 10, 41

prepositional phrases 24

    and objects 24

principal parts 6, 7, 8, 10, 12, 22, 24, 25, 27, 28, 31, 32, 43

    past 6, 7, 8, 10, 22, 24, 27

    past participle 6, 7, 8, 10, 22, 24, 25, 27, 31, 32

    present 6, 7, 8, 10, 12, 22, 24, 27

    present participle 6, 7, 8, 10, 22, 25, 27, 32

punctuation 4, 16

regular verbs 6, 7, 8, 30

state of being verbs 4, 14, 30, 31, 32, 43

subjects 4, 5, 10, 11, 12, 14, 16, 19, 25, 30, 31, 32, 36, 44

    and agreement with verbs 12, 32

    understood 5, 32

suffixes 6, 38

tenses 6, 10, 24, 30, 31–32, 34

    perfect 31, 32

    simple 31, 34

    see also principal parts

transitive verbs 14, 16, 19, 20, 22, 24, 25, 27, 29, 30

voice 30–31, 44

    active 30, 31, 44

    passive 30, 31